Restroom

Author:
Alex Woolf studied history at Essex
University, England. He is the author of over 60
books for children, including *You Wouldn't Want
to Live Without Bees!*, *You Wouldn't Want to Live
Without Vegetables!*, and *The Science of Acne and
Warts: The Itchy Truth About Skin.*

Series creator:
David Salariya was born in Dundee,
Scotland. He has illustrated a wide range of books
and has created and designed many new series
for publishers in the UK and overseas. David
established The Salariya Book Company in 1989.
He lives in Brighton, England, with his wife,
illustrator Shirley Willis, and their son, Jonathan.

Artists:
Bryan Beach
David Pavon
Caroline Romanet
Andy Rowland
Paco Sordo
Diego Vaisberg

Editor:
Jacqueline Ford

PAPER FROM
SUSTAINABLE
FORESTS

© The Salariya Book Company Ltd MMXVIII

Published in Great Britain in 2018 by
The Salariya Book Company Ltd
25 Marlborough Place, Brighton BN1 1UB

ISBN-13: 978-0-531-23142-5 (lib. bdg.) 978-0-531-23237-8 (pbk.)

Published in 2018 in the United States
by Franklin Watts
An imprint of Scholastic Inc.

A CIP catalog record for this book is available
from the Library of Congress.

Printed and bound in China.
Printed on paper from sustainable sources.
1 2 3 4 5 6 7 8 9 10 R 27 26 25 24 23 22 21 20 19 18

The Science of Poop and Farts

The Smelly Truth About Digestion

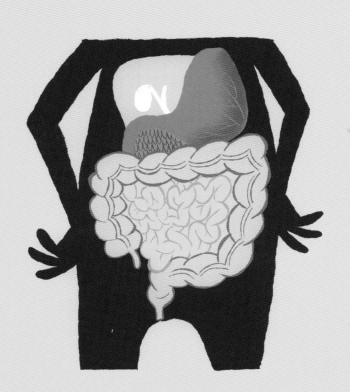

Written by
Alex Woolf

Franklin Watts®
An Imprint of Scholastic Inc.

Contents

Introduction

We all do it. Boys and girls, teachers and firefighters, doctors and astronauts, kings and queens—everyone poops. It may seem pretty gross, but it's perfectly healthy and natural. Poop (also called feces or excrement) is the solid waste that's left after we've digested our food. It's the stuff our bodies can't use for energy or growth, and it passes out of us when we go to the bathroom. So poop is really just the final product of our digestive system.

In this book we will explore how we digest our food, as well as all the strange side effects of this complex and fascinating process—including burps and farts. We will look at what happens when things go wrong, and how this affects the color, smell, and texture of our poop. We will also find out that poop is not just a smelly waste product, but can actually be useful to us.

Along the way, you will discover all sorts of fascinating facts and disgusting data, including some of the revolting things animals do with their poop!

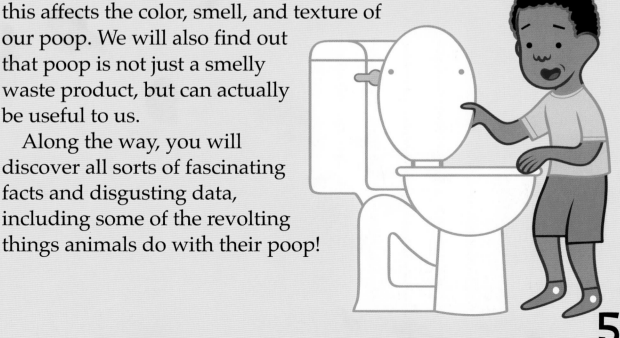

How Do We Produce Poop?

Mouth and Esophagus

In digestion, the breaking-down process of food begins in your mouth. Your teeth crush food into small, soft pieces. Saliva makes food moist and easy to swallow. When you swallow, the food goes down a tube called the esophagus and into the stomach.

The story of how we produce poop starts with the food we eat. Our bodies break down the food into useful substances that enable us to be active, to grow, and to stay healthy. This breaking-down process is called digestion, and it happens in the digestive system. The digestive system is like a long tube, nearly 29.5 feet (9 meters) in length, that starts at the mouth and ends at the anus. It is made up of several different organs, each of which helps in the process of turning food into useful substances. At the end of the process, when there are no more useful substances left, whatever is left leaves the body as poop.

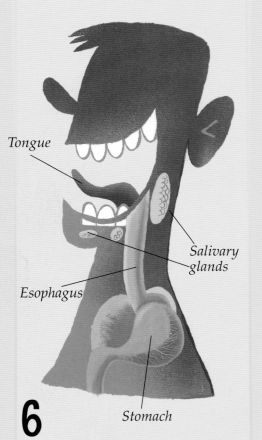

Tongue

Salivary glands

Esophagus

Stomach

Have a good journey!

Poop is made up of around 75 percent water and 25 percent solid matter. The solid matter is made up of undigestible fiber, living and dead bacteria (germs), cells, and mucus.

Fascinating Fact

Food doesn't need gravity to get to your stomach. Muscles in your esophagus push the food down, so if you wanted to, you could eat while standing on your head.

Intestines

The chyme is squirted into the small intestine, where digestive juices break it down into nutrients that are carried away to other parts of the body. The remaining waste passes to the large intestine, or colon. The colon walls absorb water from the waste, making it dry and solid (poop). The poop is stored in the rectum until you go to the bathroom.

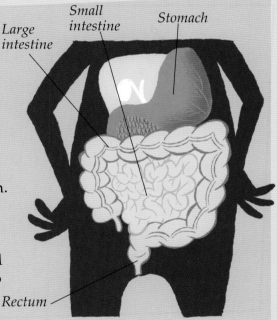

Large intestine

Small intestine

Stomach

Rectum

Stomach

When food enters the stomach, the muscles of the stomach wall churn the food around. Gastric juices mix with the food, breaking it down further. The food is turned into a thick liquid called chyme.

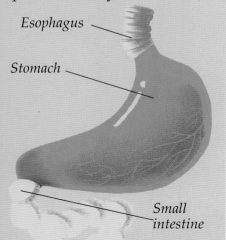

Esophagus

Stomach

Small intestine

It takes between 30 and 50 hours for food to travel from mouth to anus.

How Do Kidneys Work?

Inside each kidney are millions of tiny tubes called nephrons. As blood travels around the nephrons, waste (some water, salts, minerals, and other chemicals) is filtered out. The waste is collected at the center of the kidneys, where it is turned into urine.

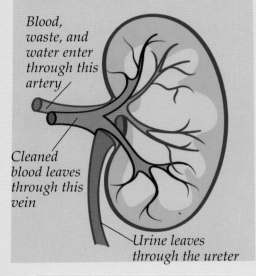

Blood, waste, and water enter through this artery

Cleaned blood leaves through this vein

Urine leaves through the ureter

If the kidneys didn't clean the blood, the waste would build up in the body and make us sick.

What Is Pee?

The body produces pee, or urine, as another way of getting rid of waste. Waste is produced when the body digests food and turns it into energy. This collects in the blood. The waste is taken out of the blood by bean-shaped organs called kidneys. You have two kidneys, one on either side of your spine. The kidneys filter the waste out of the blood, then send the cleaned blood back around the body. The kidneys also remove excess water from the blood. They turn the waste and water into urine, which then goes to the bladder, where it is stored until you need to go to the bathroom.

Some ancient Romans rinsed their mouths out with pee for whiter teeth. Yuck!

Pee gets its yellow color from a pigment in your body called urochrome. The kidneys remove bilirubin from the blood, so it ends up in your urine.

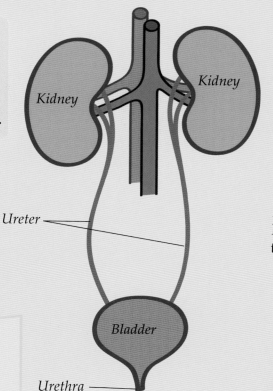

Kidney

Kidney

Ureter

Bladder

Urethra

How Does Urine Leave the Body?

The urine leaves the kidneys by a tube called a ureter, which takes it to the bladder. The bladder is a stretchy bag that slowly fills up with urine. When it's nearly full, it sends a signal to your brain and you know it's time to pee. Urine leaves your body through a tube called the urethra.

Dialysis

You can survive perfectly well with just one kidney, but you would be very sick if both kidneys stopped working properly. People whose kidneys do not work can have their blood cleaned by a dialysis machine.

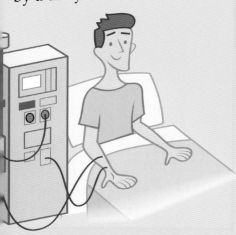

Can You Believe It?

The average adult produces 6.3 cups (1.5 liters) of urine a day. By contrast, an elephant produces 208 cups (49 L)!

Tree Shrew Toilets

The tropical pitcher plant has tube-shaped leaves that are used as toilets by the tree shrew. After the shrew has done its business, the poop it has left provides the plant with lots of nutrition.

Animal Poop

Just like humans, animals have to get rid of waste in the form of poop. Animal poop is often called dung, scat, manure, or droppings. Animals use their own poop, and the poop of other animals, in all sorts of strange and inventive ways. For example, big cats, wolves, monkeys, and wombats use their urine and poop to mark out their territory and warn other animals away. Wombats even manage to produce cube-shaped poops, so they don't roll away. The potato beetle larva uses its poop for protection. It covers itself in its own poisonous feces as a defense against predators.

Hippos spin their tails to launch their poop underwater.

Are you sure you want to do this?

Can You Believe It?

Termites grow fungus gardens inside their mounds as a source of food. They fertilize the fungus with their own droppings.

Bird-Dung Crab Spider

To protect itself from predators, the bird-dung crab spider disguises itself as—you've guessed it—bird poop! When it draws its legs in and sits very still, it mimics bird droppings in color, shape, and even smell!

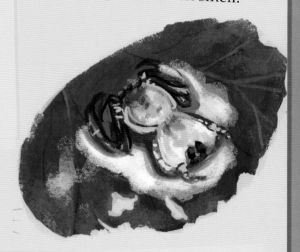

Dung beetles use the dung of larger animals as a source of food and shelter, and the larvae of some leaf beetles make homes out of their own dung.

Disgusting Data

Rabbits sometimes produce soft poop, called cecotropes, which is so nutritious, they eat it!

The average person farts, on average, 14 times a day, producing about 2 cups (0.5 L) of gas.

What Are Farts?

They can make quite a noise, and they can smell terrible! You might get embarrassed if you have one in public. But don't worry—everyone farts. Farting, or passing wind, is just a natural by-product of digestion. Farts are gas released by the body. The gas comes from several different sources. Some of it is air we have swallowed while eating. Some is gas that seeps into our intestines from our blood, and some is gas produced by the digestive process and by bacteria living in our guts. These gases can't stay in the body, so they come out as farts!

Why Do Farts Stink?

A typical fart contains mostly non-smelly gases such as nitrogen, hydrogen, carbon dioxide, and oxygen. The bad smell comes from gases containing sulfur, such as hydrogen sulfide, which make up just one percent of an average fart. If you eat lots of foods that contain sulfur, you're more likely to produce really smelly farts.

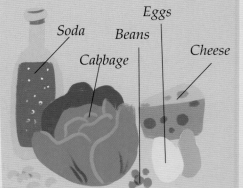

Soda

Cabbage

Beans

Eggs

Cheese

12

Why Do Farts Make That Noise?

We all know that sound. You can imitate it by blowing a raspberry. Farts make this sound when they come out by causing vibrations in the rectum. The loudness of the noise varies depending on the pressure of the gas as it escapes and the tightness of the muscles in the anus.

Is it an earthquake?

No, I think it's the beans!

Farts can travel at up to 10 feet (3 m) per second. Most are slower, taking 10 to 15 seconds to reach another person's nostrils.

Can You Believe It?

The larvae of the beaded lacewing live in termite nests, and when they get hungry they stun the termites with their farts, then eat them. One fart is powerful enough to immobilize six termites!

Beware the lacewing fart. It's silent, but deadly!

Do Some Foods Make You Fart More?

Certain foods, like beans, onions, and fried foods, release larger amounts of gas as they break down in your body. Some people have a hard time digesting foods containing lactose, a sugar found in dairy foods, and this can cause them to fart more than the usual amount.

13

Fizzy Drinks

Fizzy drinks can bring on big burps. Why? Because they contain bubbles of a gas called carbon dioxide. Other causes of burping are drinking through a straw and eating or drinking too quickly.

The sound of a burp is caused by the escaping gas making a flap of tissue at the top of the esophagus vibrate.

What Are Burps?

Have you ever accidentally made a loud burp during a meal? While you're apologizing to the other diners, you may be wondering where that came from. A burp is made of gas. When you eat, you don't swallow only food and drink, you also swallow air. Air contains gases like nitrogen and oxygen. These gases end up in your stomach. When there's too much gas in the stomach, it's forced up through the esophagus and out of the mouth as a burp. And it comes out very quickly, which is why you can't always cover your mouth in time.

Too much food?

No, too much air.

Burping Babies

When babies feed, they collect a lot of gas in their stomachs. Because they find it hard to burp on their own, this builds up and can cause them discomfort. That's why babies need to be "burped," or patted on the back, to help them release the gas.

Well done!

You're never that happy when I burp.

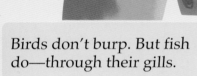

Cow Burps

Pardon me!

Cows burp a gas called methane, which contributes to global warming. Every year, cows in the U.S. burp about 50 million tons of methane. The burps of ten cows could emit enough of this gas to keep a small house heated for a year.

Birds don't burp. But fish do—through their gills.

Fascinating Fact

In some breeds of dog, such as Great Danes and Irish setters, a failure to burp can be fatal. In a condition called "bloat," gas gets trapped in their stomachs. To treat this condition, a flexible rubber tube is inserted down the dog's throat to expel the gas.

15

What Is Saliva?

In addition to helping break down food, the enzymes in saliva also fight off infections in the mouth and teeth.

It's not very pleasant when someone spits in public, or if you see a long string of drool dangling from a person's mouth. Yet spit, or saliva—the frothy liquid we produce in our mouths—plays an important role in the body. It keeps your mouth moist; it makes food wet and slippery, so it's easier to swallow; it helps your tongue taste things; and it starts the process of digestion. Saliva contains chemicals called enzymes, which start to break down food, even before it reaches the stomach. Some animals use saliva in interesting ways. Llamas, for example, will spit at other animals if they feel threatened. They can spit up to 10 feet (3 m) away.

Salivary Glands

Saliva is produced by salivary glands, which are found on the inside of each cheek and on the bottom of the mouth.

Salivary glands

How dare you take my photo!

Dry Mouth

When you are nervous or frightened, you produce less saliva, causing your mouth to be dry. Other causes of dry mouth are hot weather, drinking too little water, and heavy exercise.

The average person produces just under 4 cups (1 L) of saliva a day—enough to fill two bathtubs a year.

Can You Believe It?

The spitting spider produces a substance containing venom and a sticky kind of silk. It spits this at its prey, paralyzing it. The spider can then eat its victim at its leisure.

Swift Saliva

Some species of swift use their saliva to build their nests. The saliva hardens into a glue that holds the nest together. This sticky saliva is used to make the Chinese delicacy bird's nest soup.

What Are Diarrhea and Vomiting?

What Causes Diarrhea?

Diarrhea may be caused by germs such as viruses and bacteria. These can get into your body through contaminated food or drink, or through contact with an infected person or animal.

To prevent diarrhea, always wash your hands with soap after going to the bathroom and before you prepare or eat any food.

Sometimes you might get a pain in your stomach and an urgent need to go to the bathroom. When you go, your poop is runny or watery. This is diarrhea. It happens because you have eaten some food that your body needs to get rid of quickly. The food may have gone bad, or perhaps it contains something poisonous or something to which you are allergic. Normally it takes between 12 and 40 hours for food to pass through the intestines. When you have diarrhea, the food is rushed through your intestines much faster than normal. Bacteria prevent the water in your food from being absorbed, which is why the poop, when it comes out, is soft and runny.

Emergency! Get out of my way!

Restroom

Vomiting

Uggghh! Sometimes your body has to get rid of bad or poisonous food even before it reaches the intestines—when it's still in the stomach. Vomiting is a powerful, violent urge that you just can't stop, often leading to a mess on the floor.

What Happens When You Vomit?

When you vomit, a ring of muscle at the top of the stomach relaxes, and stomach muscles force the food into the esophagus and then up and out through the mouth. The vomit tastes horrible because the food has been mixed with the acidic juices in your stomach.

The fulmar is a seabird. When another bird tries to eat a fulmar chick, to protect itself the chick will vomit a slimy substance that sticks to the predator's feathers.

Helpful Hint

Diarrhea makes you lose fluids and can cause dehydration. If you get diarrhea, make sure you drink lots of fluids.

What Is Constipation?

Constipation has many causes, including a lack of fiber in your diet, insufficient exercise, and anxiety. Even a change of routine, like going on vacation, can cause constipation.

Toilet Terrors

When people feel stressed, for example before a test, they might become constipated. A fear of public bathrooms can cause some people to suppress the urge to poop.

Sometimes you feel like you want to poop, but you can't. Or doing it might be difficult and need a lot more pushing than normal. When it comes out, the feces is often small, hard, and lumpy. You might have a feeling that not everything came out. These are all signs of constipation. Almost everyone gets constipated at some point in their lives, and it's usually not serious. Constipation is the opposite of diarrhea—food stays in the intestines for longer than normal, so more water is absorbed, making the poop dry and hard.

Poop Chart

The Bristol stool chart was developed to show the different kinds of poop. Poop varies in shape and texture depending on how long it takes food to pass through your intestines. This chart can help doctors diagnose digestive problems.

 Type 1: Separate hard lumps—very constipated

 *Type 2: Lumpy and sausage-like—slightly constipated*

 *Type 3: Sausage-like with cracks in the surface—normal*

 *Type 4: A smooth, soft sausage or snake—normal*

 *Type 5: Soft blobs with clear-cut edges—normal*

 *Type 6: Mushy with ragged edges—diarrhea*

 *Type 7: Liquid with no solid pieces—diarrhea*

Fabulous Fiber

One cause of constipation is not eating enough fiber. Fiber is found in fruits, vegetables, and whole-grain cereals. It is bulky and helps food move easily through the intestines.

Call a doctor if you see blood in your poop, if you have severe pain when you poop, or if your constipation has lasted for more than two weeks.

Helpful Hint

If you are constipated:
- drink lots of water
- eat more fruit and vegetables
- eat prunes and bran cereal

Digestive Problems

What IS Heartburn?

Heartburn, or acid reflux, happens when stomach acid escapes into the esophagus. Because the esophagus is not as well protected as the stomach, this can produce a burning sensation in the chest and throat.

You're breathing fire!

It may just be heartburn.

Why doesn't stomach acid damage your stomach? Because the stomach's lining is coated with mucus, which protects it from the acid.

Most of the time, if your digestive system is working properly, you should feel no discomfort at all after eating a meal. However, sometimes, things can go wrong. Perhaps you feel uncomfortably full or bloated, or suffer a burning sensation above your stomach (heartburn). You may feel sick. You may burp a lot, or even vomit. These are all signs of indigestion. Causes can include eating greasy or spicy foods, eating too much, eating too quickly, exercising too soon after eating, or stress.

Eaten too much again?

What Are Food Allergies?

Sometimes the body's immune system (which provides resistance to infection) reacts to particular foods. It might cause itching or swelling inside the mouth or throat, an itchy red rash, swelling of the face, or vomiting. This is called an allergic reaction. People with serious food allergies should carry medicine with them to stop an allergic reaction.

Peanuts

Fish

Milk

Shellfish

Eggs

Up to 1 in 12 children have a food allergy, and 40 percent of them have a severe reaction. The good news is, many children outgrow their allergies.

What Is a Hiccup?

A hiccup is a quick, involuntary intake of air. It happens when a muscle called the diaphragm contracts sharply. Hiccups can happen if you irritate your stomach by eating too much food. The "hick!" sound is caused by the sudden closure of your vocal chords.

Hiccup "Cures"

Sip ice-cold water

Hold your breath

Bite on a lemon

Can You Believe It?

The longest bout of hiccups lasted 68 years. Charles Osborne (1894–1991) suffered nonstop hiccups from 1922 to 1990.

Hiccup!

Hiccup!

23

A Healthy Diet

If you become very overweight, it can be bad for your health. To stay healthy, we should limit our intake of foods that are high in sugar and carbohydrates.

Proteins

Proteins are the building blocks of the body. They help your body grow strong and repair damage such as cuts, bruises, and broken bones. For vegetarians and vegans, nuts, lentils, and chickpeas are good sources of protein.

Your diet is everything you eat and drink. A healthy diet (also called a balanced diet) provides you with all the nutrients you need. There are four main groups of nutrients: proteins (found in meat, fish, eggs, and nuts); vitamins and minerals (fresh fruit and vegetables); carbohydrates (potatoes, rice, bread, and sugary foods); and fats (fried foods, dairy products, and nuts). Many people are attracted to foods that are high in carbohydrates and fats, such as fried and sugary foods, because they find them delicious. If you eat too much of these high-energy foods, your body will store the extra Calories as fat.

Will steak make my leg better?

It's a balanced meal.

It needs to be balanced with a serious amount of cake!

24

Most doctors think we should try to eat at least five portions of fresh fruit and vegetables a day.

Carbohydrates and Fats

Carbohydrates are the most important source of energy for your body. There are two main kinds: starch (found in potatoes, rice, and bread) and sugars (found in fruit, vegetables, milk, and dairy products). Fats also provide us with energy, as well as other important chemicals that our bodies need.

Starchy foods give you a steady amount of energy.

Sugary foods give you quick bursts of energy!

Vitamins and Minerals

Your body needs only tiny amounts of vitamins and minerals, but they are essential for keeping you fit and healthy.

Oranges contain vitamin C, which will help my body fight off colds.

Fascinating Fact

Energy in food is called Calories. By exercising, you can burn off Calories. It would take more than an hour of walking to burn all the Calories in a slice of cake with frosting.

Can Poop Be Useful?

Animal dung has been used as building material, cooking fuel, and to make paper. Conservationists examine dung to learn about the health and whereabouts of animals.

Feces Fertilizer

Farmers have been using animal poop as a fertilizer for thousands of years. They use dung from horses, cattle, sheep, pigs, and chickens, as well as guano from bats and birds. Even panda poop has been used—to fertilize tea plants in China.

We usually think of poop as a waste product—something to get rid of down the toilet. Yet it can be a surprisingly useful substance. For example, farmers use animal dung, or manure, to fertilize their crops. The manure contains lots of nutrients that make the soil more fertile. Poop is also a source of energy. It can be converted into biogas, which can provide heat and electricity. Biogas can be turned into biomethane to power cars. And archaeologists study ancient poop to learn about the diet and lifestyle of our early ancestors.

At least it doesn't smell anymore.

Hmm—a faint smell of pandas.

Samples of Ancient Poop

26

Poop Power

The gas from animal poop is warmed in airtight containers. Bacteria then turns the poop into a fuel called biogas, which can be burned to generate heat and power. The poop of 500 cows can create enough electricity to power 100 homes.

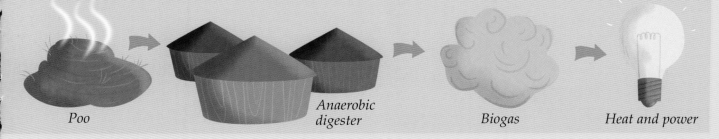

Poo

Anaerobic digester

Biogas

Heat and power

Elephant Dung Paper

A company in Thailand makes paper products from elephant dung. Since the dung is mainly fiber, it is an excellent material for papermaking. A single elephant produces around 110 pounds (50 kilograms) of dung a day, which can make about 115 sheets of paper.

Eat up, I've run out of paper!

Flying squirrel dung tea is used in Chinese medicine to cure stomach pain.

Disgusting Data

During the 18th century, tanners would use a blend of human urine and dog poop to make leather. They would knead this smelly mixture into animal hides until they became soft and easy to shape.

What Happens to Poop?

P oop contains germs, some of which can damage our health. That's why it's very important that we dispose of it safely. In the developed world, most people have flushing toilets that wash our waste safely away. This is not always the case in the developing world; in some remote villages, people must go to the bathroom in the open, and germs from their feces can contaminate local water supplies. This can endanger the health of those who use the water, and also harm wildlife.

Sewage Treatment

After poop has been flushed, it is carried through pipes to a sewage treatment plant. Here, it is filtered and treated to clean it of impurities. Purified liquid waste is released into waterways. The remaining solid waste (sludge) is dumped, or dried and sold to farmers as fertilizer.

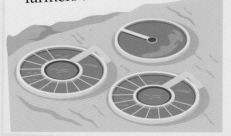

28

How Does Nature Deal With Poop?

Time to start a new island.

In nature, poop often benefits the environment. For example, sea cucumbers excrete a mineral used to build coral reefs. Worm poop helps fertilize the soil. And parrot fish excrete sand. After thousands of years, this forms the white sandy beaches of Caribbean islands.

Spreading Seeds

The tambaqui fish of the Amazon help to disperse tree seeds in the rain forest. The fish eat the seeds that fall from the trees, then excrete them so they can sprout somewhere else.

The trees feed me, so I do my part to help them!

Animal poop can be dangerous. Dog and cat poop can cause diseases in humans if not disposed of safely. And cow dung pollutes the atmosphere and waterways.

Fascinating Fact

The average person:
- excretes almost a ton of poop a year
- visits the bathroom 2,500 times a year
- spends about three years of his or her life on the toilet

Glossary

Allergic reaction A damaging response by the body to a substance.

Anaerobic digester A tank in which bacteria break down organic matter in the absence of oxygen.

Anus The opening at the end of the digestive tract through which poop leaves the body.

Artery Any of the tubes that carry blood from the heart to the other parts of the body.

Bacteria Microscopic organisms, some of which can cause disease.

Biogas A gaseous fuel such as methane, produced by the breakdown of organic matter in the absence of oxygen.

Biomethane A purified form of biogas that can be used as natural gas.

Carbohydrate A substance found in foods such as potatoes, pasta, and sugar, that gives the body energy.

Conservationist Someone who helps preserve wildlife and the environment.

Dehydration A state in which a person has lost a large amount of water.

Esophagus The tube connecting the throat to the stomach.

Excrete Expel waste.

Feces Waste matter discharged from the intestines after food has been digested. Another word for poop.

Fiber A substance found in foods such as cereals, which resists digestion and helps move digested food through the intestines.

Gastric juices Acidic fluids produced by the stomach for digesting food.

Global warming A gradual increase in the temperature of Earth's atmosphere caused by increased levels of carbon dioxide and other pollutants.

Guano Bird and bat poop.

Intestine The lower part of the digestive system, from the end of the stomach to the anus.

Larva The immature form of an insect.

Manure Animal dung used as fertilizer.

Minerals Substances such as iron and calcium needed by the body for good health.

Mucus A slimy substance produced by the body for protection and lubrication.

Nutrient A substance that provides nourishment needed for growth and a healthy life.

Protein A type of chemical essential to all living organisms.

Rectum The final section of the large intestine, ending at the anus.

Salivary glands Organs inside the cheeks and under the tongue that secrete saliva into the mouth.

Sewage Solid and liquid waste carried in sewers.

Stool Another word for poop.

Vegan A person who doesn't eat or use animal products.

Vein Any of the tubes in the body that carry blood toward the heart.

Virus A tiny organism that can reproduce and grow only when inside living cells. Viruses cause diseases such as the common cold and gastroenteritis (stomach flu).

Vitamins Substances that are essential for normal growth and nutrition. We need to include them in our diet because they cannot be produced by the body.

Index